If I Were a Cowboy

by Eric Braun   illustrated by Mick Reid

Special thanks to our adviser for his expertise:

Terry Flaherty, Ph.D., Professor of English
Minnesota State University, Mankato

PICTURE WINDOW BOOKS
a capstone imprint

dreamBIG

Editors: Shelly Lyons and Jennifer Besel
Designer: Tracy Davies
Art Director: Nathan Gassman
Production Specialist: Jane Klenk

The illustrations in this book were created with watercolor and colored pencil.

Picture Window Books
151 Good Counsel Drive
P.O. Box 669
Mankato, MN 56002-0669
877-845-8392
www.picturewindowbooks.com

Printed in the United States of America in North Mankato, Minnesota.

092009
005618CGS10

Library of Congress Cataloging-in-Publication Data
Braun, Eric.
If I were a cowboy / by Eric Braun; illustrated by Mick Reid.
p. cm. — (Dream big!)
Includes index.
ISBN 978-1-4048-5531-1 (library binding)
1. Cowboys—Juvenile literature. 2. West (U.S.)—Social life and
customs—Juvenile literature. I. Title.
F596.B825 2010
978'.034—dc22   2009024066

If I were a cowboy, I would herd cattle and take care of them.

If I were a cowboy, I would ride a galloping horse. I would feel the horse's muscles moving beneath me. We would race across the open land.

A female who takes care of cattle and horses is called a cowgirl.

6

If I were a cowboy, I would wake up before sunrise. I would rub my eyes and eat breakfast in the dark. Then it would be time to work.

If I were a cowboy, I would wear tough pants and boots. They would keep me safe on the trail. My hat would protect me from the sun.

When riding horses, cowboys often wear leather chaps over their pants. Chaps protect cowboys' legs from scratches and other dangers. The leggings also help cowboys keep warm when it's cold on the trail.

If I were a cowboy, I would lead cattle to a grassy field. The dogs would help me herd the cattle. They would yip and run alongside us.

Ya! Get on!

Cowboys have to move their cattle often. It can be hard for one cowboy to get dozens of cattle to move at the same time. Trained dogs help cowboys by running beside the cattle to keep the animals in line.

11

If I were a cowboy, I would fix a fence. The fence would keep my animals together. It would also protect them from dangerous animals, such as wolves and coyotes.

If I were a cowboy, I would learn more about caring for my cattle. I would use my computer to find information.

Today, computers can help cowboys do their jobs. Cowboys can use computers to keep track of money. They can also learn more about their cattle and how best to take care of them.

If I were a cowboy, I would care for a sick cow. Its ears would twitch as I gave it a pill. I would comfort the cow by petting its side and talking softly. The medicine would help.

That's a good girl.

If I were a cowboy, I would fork hay from a wagon. The hungry animals would eat the hay. I would eat my own lunch. It would be even tastier than hay!

If I were a cowboy, I would ride in a rodeo. I would swing a rope over my head. I would love being a cowboy!

Yee-haw!

How do you get to be a Cowboy?

People who want to be cowboys or cowgirls have to learn to ride a horse. They need to know a lot about animals so they can take care of them. Cowboys also need to know how to fix machines, such as tractors. Cowboys spend most of their time outside, so people who want to be cowboys should love the outdoors. Cowboys usually work on a ranch. Ranches have lots of land for cattle and horses. If you own your own ranch, you will need to learn how to run a business, too.

Glossary

cattle—cows

gallop—running at full speed; when a horse gallops, all four of its hooves leave the ground at once.

herd—to make a group of animals, such as cattle, move together

rodeo—a contest for cowboys and cowgirls to compare their skills in riding wild horses and roping cattle

trail—a track or path that people follow

To Learn More

More Books to Read

Gordon, Sharon. *At Home on the Ranch.* New York: Marshall Cavendish Benchmark, 2006.

Knowlton, Laurie Lazzaro. *Cowgirl Alphabet.* Gretna, La.: Pelican, 2009.

Urbigkit, Cat. *Cattle Kids: A Year on the Western Range.* Honesdale, Penn.: Boyds Mills Press, 2007.

Internet Sites

FactHound offers a safe, fun way to find Internet sites related to this book. All of the sites on FactHound have been researched by our staff.

Here's all you do:

Visit *www.facthound.com*

FactHound will fetch the best sites for you!

Index

Look for all of the books in the Dream Big! series: